P9-DVX-508

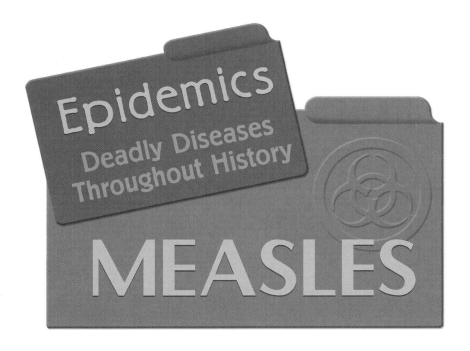

MAXINE ROSALER

Epidemics
Deadly Diseases
Throughout History

MEASLES

The Rosen Publishing Group, Inc.
New York

Published in 2005 by The Rosen Publishing Group, Inc.
29 East 21st Street, New York, NY 10010

Library of Congress Cataloging-in-Publication Data

Rosaler, Maxine.
Measles/by Maxine Rosaler.—1st ed.
        p. cm.—(Epidemics)
Includes bibliographical references and index.
ISBN 1-4042-0256-0 (library binding)
1. Measles—Juvenile literature.
I. Title. II. Series.
RA644.M5R67 2005
614.5′23—dc22

                                                    2004014113

Manufactured in the United States of America

Cover image: A colored electron micrograph of a budding
measles virus

CONTENTS

A young girl with measles looks out from her quarantined room. The practice of quarantining, or isolating sick people to prevent them from infecting others, began during the fourteenth century. Ships arriving in Venice, Italy, were required to sit at anchor for forty days before landing. In fact, the word "quarantine" comes from the Latin word *quaresma*, meaning "forty." Quarantine remains one of the most effective ways of limiting the spread of disease.

INTRODUCTION

Up until the 1960s, measles was simply a fact of life in the United States and most of the developed world. Each year about half a million people, mostly children, would come down with an illness whose symptoms were usually no worse than those of a bad cold, except for a rash that would spread over the victim's body in little red spots. Because it was known that a person developed immunity to measles after the first outbreak and never became sick with it again, parents would often send their children over to a sick neighbor's house in order for them to deliberately catch measles and get the illness over with. It was better, parents and doctors thought, for people to get measles in childhood, when they were otherwise strong and healthy.

Since people would sometimes even go out of their way to get measles, the disease developed the reputation for being harmless, at least among children.

This impression was in many ways mistaken. Every year a small percentage of the many people who caught measles become seriously ill and died of it, just as today a small number of adults and children die during the annual flu epidemics that most of us take in stride. A closely related malady called the German measles, or rubella, was a frequent cause of serious birth defects in babies born from pregnant women who came down with the disease.

If we look deeper into the past, we will discover that measles has been one of history's deadliest killers. Carried to the Americas by European colonists who were immune to the disease or only slightly harmed by it, measles (together with smallpox and other diseases) wiped out entire Native American populations and changed the course of history.

1

WHAT IS MEASLES?

Measles is a highly contagious disease. It is caused by a virus—an extremely tiny organism that can only reproduce itself by residing within living cells. Humans are the only living creatures who can develop measles, and they can only get it if they are exposed to the measles virus.

The most common way that people get infected with the disease is by breathing in tiny droplets of water vapor containing the measles virus. An uninfected person can get measles just by breathing the air in a room that was previously occupied by an infected person. The measles virus can live in the air for two hours after an infected person leaves the room. People can also get measles if they have direct contact with fluid from the nose or mouth of an infected person.

Once introduced into a person's respiratory system, the measles virus proceeds to attach itself to the lining of the airways. Drawing energy from this new host, the virus begins to multiply and spread throughout the body.

Symptoms of Measles

About ten to fourteen days after exposure to the measles virus, people infected with measles will get a rash, high fever, cough, runny nose, and watery eyes. The eye symptoms can develop into conjunctivitis (pink eye), a condition that causes swelling and redness of the eye, tearing, and sensitivity to light. The skin rash often takes the form of bright red spots that are distinct and separate from each other. They may multiply so rapidly, however, that they appear to be a solid red mass. The rash usually starts behind the ears and along the hairline, and then quickly spreads to the rest of the face, moving downward to the rest of the body. In addition to this red rash, light spots resembling grains of salt may appear on the inside of the patient's cheeks near the back of the mouth. Doctors call these Koplik's spots. These typical measles symptoms last for one to two weeks.

Most people recover from measles within ten to fourteen days. After they are well again, they are no longer contagious, which means they can no longer infect other people with the disease. In addition, people who have had measles develop an immunity to it—they will never catch measles again, even if someone with the disease sneezes or coughs right in their face.

Complications of Measles

For most people who are otherwise healthy and well nourished, measles is not a serious illness. However, a small percentage of those who get the disease suffer complications that can be painful or even deadly. These complications are the reason the U.S. Centers for Disease Control and Prevention (or the CDC, which is in charge of tracking and controlling

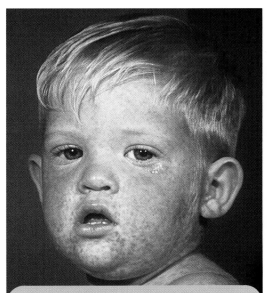

This 1963 picture of a boy with measles shows the characteristic rash caused by the disease. Measles were once so common that in 2004, any person over age 55 is assumed to have had it in the past, before the MMR inoculation was widespread.

the spread of disease in the United States) strongly recommends that all children be vaccinated against measles. Vaccination involves the injection of a weakened form of the measles virus into a person's body. Following the injection, the virus grows and causes a harmless infection in the vaccinated person, who shows very few, if any, symptoms. The person's immune system fights the mild infection caused by the weakened measles virus and an immunity to the disease develops that lasts throughout that person's life. Complications of measles can include:

- **Ear infections:** Most people have experienced at least one ear infection in their lives. These are sometimes painful and occur when germs multiply in the ear.

- **Pneumonia:** This is an infection or inflammation of lung tissue. Pneumonia can occur in many different diseases and can be mild or very serious, even fatal.

- **Bronchitis:** Bronchitis is an inflammation and congestion of the bronchial tubes that lead into the lungs.

- **Diarrhea:** This condition is characterized by frequent and loose bowel movements.

While most often thought of as a source of embarrassment or bathroom humor, diarrhea can in fact be a very serious, even fatal disorder. Throughout history, untreated diarrhea has killed millions of people. It is still a deadly disease in parts of the world where good health care, proper sanitation, and clean water are unavailable.

◉ **Seizures:** Seizures are random firings of the cells in the central nervous system—the body's electrical and communication system that controls sensation, movement, and thinking. Seizures can be so tiny that they pass completely unnoticed, or they can be so strong and powerful that they can cause wild, jerky movements that affect the entire body.

◉ **Hearing loss:** Various degrees of deafness can result from brain damage caused by measles.

In addition, measles can lead to an enlarged spleen, swollen lymph nodes, liver inflammation, and eye ulcers. Measles causes ear infections in nearly one out of every ten infected children. As many as one out of twenty children with measles also develops pneumonia. About one child in every 1,000 who is infected with the measles virus will also come down with encephalitis. For every 1,000 children who get measles, one to two will die from it. Pregnant women who develop measles are at a higher risk for miscarriage (death of the fetus) or premature birth in which the baby is born weeks or even months before its due date.

Why does measles sometimes cause all these complications? Part of the answer has to do with an early symptom of measles that is not visible to the naked eye. The first thing the measles virus does—even before it causes a runny nose, fever, or rash—is attack its victim's immune system, which has the job of fighting off disease. Measles injures and kills white blood cells, the body's first line of defense against germs. As a result, people who have measles have fewer defenses against other infections, so they can become sick with other illnesses while they are fighting measles.

Who Gets Measles?

There are certain people for whom measles poses an unusually grave danger. Infants and the very young can be vulnerable to it because their immune systems are not yet fully developed (most children do not receive the measles vaccine until they are between twelve to fifteen months old, though

In this 2004 photo, a young Sudanese boy living in a war-torn area shows a bloated belly, one of the characteristics of severe malnutrition. Malnutrition is caused by a lack of vitamins and minerals. Malnourished children often have weakened immune systems, making them more likely to contract diseases like measles.

infants are generally protected against the disease for the first six to eight months of their lives by immunity passed on from their mothers). The elderly are also at risk because their immune systems are often weakened by age and other diseases.

People of any age who are weakened by malnutrition can also become gravely sick with measles. For this reason, measles continues to pose a threat in poor countries where there are large groups of people who do not get enough to eat. Malnutrition does not just mean not getting enough food. It also means not getting enough high-quality food—food with the vitamins, minerals, and proteins that boost the immune system, fight disease, and promote good health. Many poor people around the world suffer from malnutrition. In addition, health care in poor countries is not as good as it is in developed countries, which further increases the dangerous effects of measles. In the rural areas of many poor countries, between 5 and 10 percent of children who get measles die of it.

Measles is usually considered to be a disease of childhood. Adults seldom get it, for the simple reason that a person can get measles only once, and since the measles virus is so contagious and widespread, most people catch it early in life. However, older people who have not been exposed to the virus and have not been vaccinated against it are just as likely to catch the disease as children are. Since vaccination against measles has been extremely effective, most cases of measles that occur worldwide involve people who have not received the vaccine.

In wealthy and developed countries like the United States, where good nutrition and good health care are the norm, most people are vaccinated against measles by the age of eighteen months. As a result of the vaccine, measles has been nearly wiped out in the United States and outbreaks are very rare.

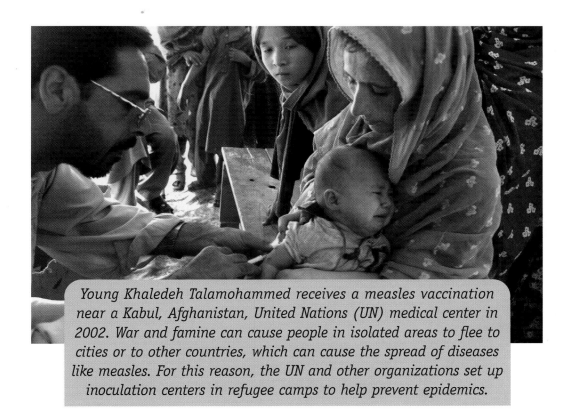

Young Khaledeh Talamohammed receives a measles vaccination near a Kabul, Afghanistan, United Nations (UN) medical center in 2002. War and famine can cause people in isolated areas to flee to cities or to other countries, which can cause the spread of diseases like measles. For this reason, the UN and other organizations set up inoculation centers in refugee camps to help prevent epidemics.

How Many People Get Measles?

Before the measles vaccine was available, nearly all children came down with measles by the time they were fifteen years old. An average of 530,000 cases a year were reported in the United States during the ten years before most people started getting the vaccine in 1963, and an average of 450 people died every year due to the disease. Now, thanks to the measles vaccine, the number of measles cases each year is a fraction of what it was then. In 2001, there were 116 reported cases of measles in the United

States, with one fatality. However, we should not assume that children today are entirely safe from the threat of measles. In 1989 and 1990, there was a large increase in the number of measles cases in the United States, partly because many parents failed to have their preschool-age children vaccinated.

Treatment

For uncomplicated cases of measles, doctors recommend rest, plenty of fluids, and fever-lowering drugs. Sometimes a humidifier or a steam kettle can help relieve the swelling of the windpipe that often goes along with measles and makes breathing difficult. Since measles is caused by a virus and not bacteria, the bacteria-fighting drugs called antibiotics are ineffective against it. However, antibiotics can be used to treat some of the infections that are the complications of measles, such as conjunctivitis. The more serious complications of measles are treated with a wide variety of drugs and, in some cases, even surgery.

2

THE HISTORY OF MEASLES

Like many other epidemic diseases, measles is probably part of the price we pay for civilization. The domestication of animals (the adaptation of them for human use), the growth of great cities, and the development of international trade all contributed to the spread of infectious diseases.

The Origins of the Measles Virus

Some scientists believe that the domestication of animals may have contributed to the spread of disease, since many human diseases resemble diseases found in farm animals. Daily contact with farm animals gave animal germs a chance to infect human beings. The animal illnesses that most closely resemble measles are canine distemper and

This fifteenth-century image shows a street of shops in a medieval village. The construction of crowded cities made it easier for disease to spread from person to person in medieval Europe.

rinderpest. Canine distemper is a contagious, incurable, often fatal viral disease that affects the respiratory, gastrointestinal, and central nervous systems of dogs. Rinderpest is a highly infectious viral disease that can destroy entire populations of cattle and buffalo.

The emergence of big cities also helped diseases spread among our ancestors. Diseases like measles are spread by person-to-person contact, and the sick are usually contagious for only a short time. In a small village, measles quickly runs out of people to infect and soon dies out. In a large, crowded city, in which babies are born every day, new people are continuously settling, and citizens live closely packed together, the disease never runs out of potential victims. Measles probably began with the start of urban life in the Middle East around 3000 BC.

While diseases such as measles could ravage large cities, long-distance trade also allowed them to travel from city to city. Germs and viruses hitched a ride with the sailors on a ship or with camel drivers of a desert caravan, and at their destination found a whole new human population to infect.

Measles Outbreaks in Ancient Times

The writings of ancient times contain many references to sudden outbreaks of disease. In most cases, we cannot be sure exactly what these diseases were.

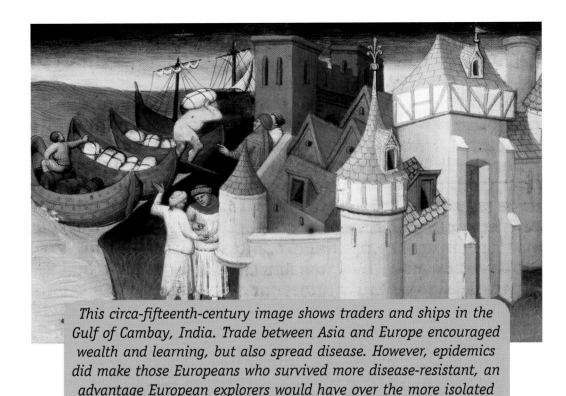

This circa-fifteenth-century image shows traders and ships in the Gulf of Cambay, India. Trade between Asia and Europe encouraged wealth and learning, but also spread disease. However, epidemics did make those Europeans who survived more disease-resistant, an advantage European explorers would have over the more isolated Native Americans.

Some historians believe that a plague that killed a large part of the Athenian army in 430 to 429 BC was measles. If this is true, one reason the epidemic turned out to be so deadly might have been because the Athenians had never been exposed to measles before. The outbreak could have been made more deadly if whoever brought measles to the Athenians also brought other new and foreign diseases along with it. We now know that measles weakens the immune system. This means that if a measles infection is coupled with another disease, the combination can cause a much more dangerous and severe illness than either disease operating by itself.

It is thought that measles may have been behind the mysterious epidemic that killed half of a Carthaginian army that invaded Sicily in the fifth century BC. That epidemic changed the course of history, turning a likely victory for the Carthaginians into a stunning defeat. Since they were the greatest enemies of the early Romans, a measles epidemic among the Carthaginians may have indirectly led to the rise of the Roman Empire.

Measles and Smallpox— A Deadly Pair

One reason that measles was so dangerous in ancient times was that it was often accompanied by another, even more deadly illness called smallpox. Smallpox, like measles, is a viral infection. It is usually considered to be a much more serious illness than measles. When the inhabitants of an ancient city or the soldiers in an ancient army encampment were infected with measles, the illness would end up weakening their immune systems. If, at the same time as or shortly after the measles infection people were also exposed to the smallpox virus, a very large number of them would catch smallpox and die. This may be

Many scientists believe that mankind's most common diseases originate from farm animals. According to this theory, our distant ancestors, who lived by hunting wild animals and gathering wild plants, were relatively free of infectious diseases. Originally, the animal forms of these germs were unable to infect human beings. Instead, they were designed to infect a particular species. But germs, like all living things, evolve, or change a little from generation to generation. Since a generation for many germs is only about twenty minutes, germs can evolve very quickly. Following the widespread domestication of animals, such as cows and sheep, frequent everyday contact between human beings and farm animals gave many animal germs

This detail of a limestone carving from circa 2492 to 2345 BC shows a herdsman leading a bull. Animal domestication was one of the earliest innovations of ancient societies.

the opportunity to evolve into agents that could infect human beings. This table shows some common farm animals and a few of the human diseases that may have been passed on from them.

ANIMAL	FIRST DOMESTICATED	DISEASES
Cattle	4000 BC	Measles, smallpox, tuberculosis
Pigs	4000 BC	Influenza (flu)
Dogs	12,000–8000 BC	Pertussis (whooping cough)
Sheep, goats	7000 BC	Anthrax
Chickens	7000 BC	Cholera

the reason why measles was a mere annoyance for one group of people, while for another group it could be a deadly plague that would wipe out a large segment of the population.

Historians of medicine suspect that measles and smallpox were the cause of several ancient plagues that decimated large groups of people in densely populated areas. In large communities where measles and smallpox were endemic (where, at any given time, at least a few people were sick with these diseases), a rise in measles infection was often followed by a rise in smallpox deaths, as well as an increase in the number of deaths from other illnesses.

Measles in the Medieval Era

By the medieval era, or Middle Ages (fifth to the fifteenth centuries AD), measles is thought to have appeared in India, China, Japan, and Africa. According to medieval medical records, measles was very much a part of everyday life in these countries. We know measles was endemic in the Near East and India by the seventh century because medical textbooks written in Arabic and Sanskrit give precise descriptions of measles and recommend treatments for it.

In England during the Middle Ages, the word "mezils" was already being used to describe the illness we know today as measles, although the term was also applied to other diseases that caused rashes. By the 1700s, physicians began to observe the weakening effect measles had on the immune system. They soon recognized that measles could lead to other, even more dangerous diseases and infections.

Measles in the Age of Exploration

During the final years of the fifteenth century, European explorers began their voyages of discovery to the New World and their conquest of the Americas. The Europeans arrived with special advantages that helped them impose their will on Native Americans. While some Native American peoples, such as the Aztecs of Mexico and the Incas of Peru, had complex urban societies, their tools of warfare were inferior to those of the Europeans. The Europeans had guns, steel, and horses.

But by far the most lethal weapon that the Europeans wielded against the Native Americans was one that they were not even aware they possessed: their germs. In the end, germs did far more than guns and armor to help the Spanish, Portuguese, French, and English clear the land of its original inhabitants, defeat their enemies, and establish their empires in the New World.

The germs that the European explorers and conquerors brought with them to the Americas in the early sixteenth century were deadly to Native Americans who had never been exposed to them before. Europeans had developed immunities to these germs centuries before. As a result, diseases that were a mere nuisance to Europeans, such as chicken pox, smallpox, and measles, wiped out entire communities of Native Americans. Ultimately, diseases from Europe are thought to have wiped out up to 95 percent of the native population of America.

Why did the Old World germs kill so many Native Americans, while the germs of the Native Americans ended up killing relatively few Europeans? The answer is that the Europeans simply had more germs to spread

3000 BC
Measles may have first appeared with the growth of cities in the Middle East.

Seventh century AD
Earliest references to measles.

Tenth century
Measles is first scientifically described and differentiated from smallpox by Persian-born physician Ibn Razi.

Late fifteenth–early sixteenth centuries
Measles is introduced to the New World by European explorers, devastating many Native American populations.

1757
Scottish physician Francis Home demonstrates that measles is caused by an infectious agent present in the blood of patients.

1846
Danish physician Peter Panum studies a measles outbreak in the Faroe Islands and shows that the disease is acquired solely by direct trans-mission. He also describes the measles' incuba-tion period and lifetime immu-nity from it.

1941
In the United States, 894,134 cases of measles are reported, resulting in 2,250 deaths.

1954

John F. Enders and Thomas C. Peebles report the first successful isolation and propagation of the measles virus in human and monkey kidney cells. This leads to Enders's development of a live measles vaccine in the late 1950s

1966–1968

Almost 20 million doses of measles vaccine are given to children in the United States, and the number of measles cases plummets.

1989

Large increase in measles cases indicates failure of the vaccine to provide lifelong immunity and leads to the introduction of a measles booster shot.

2001

The lowest number of measles cases—116—ever is recorded in the United States, resulting in only one death.

2003

Worldwide, there are estimated to be 30 million measles cases and 700,000 deaths each year. More than half of the deaths occur in Africa. In countries and regions of the world that are able to keep vaccination coverage high—including North America—measles is very rare.

1978

Doctors in the United States begin giving children a combined vaccine that protects against measles, mumps, and rubella.

than the Native Americans did. The three continents of Europe, Asia, and Africa had been linked by trading routes for centuries. For hundreds of years, European sailors and traders came into contact with the germs found in these continents and brought them home with them. As a result, Europeans had long since become exposed to a wide range of illnesses that were no longer life-threatening. So, in addition to carrying with them to the New World the infectious diseases that were indigenous, or native, to the European continent, Europeans also carried with them infectious diseases from Asia and much of Africa.

The first-known measles epidemic in America occurred in 1517, in Columbus's first New World settlement, Hispaniola (present-day Santo Domingo, capital of the Dominican Republic). Major measles epidemics were also recorded in central Mexico in 1531, 1563, and 1595. During the sixteenth century, measles is thought to have killed two-thirds of the population of Cuba. It began spreading through South America in the 1530s. The devastating effect that measles can have on a population that has never before been exposed to it was illustrated in more recent history when the disease was accidentally introduced to the Fiji Islands in 1875. Around 40,000 Fiji islanders, a quarter of the total population of the islands, died in this measles epidemic.

3

THE SEARCH FOR THE MEASLES VIRUS

Today we know a great deal about measles. We know that it is caused by a microscopic organism called a virus. Scientists have managed to grow the measles virus outside the human body, which has enabled them to develop a vaccine that prevents people from catching measles. We have learned a great deal about the way measles works and how it makes people sick. None of this knowledge came quickly or easily. It was the product of many years of research.

Early Attempts to Fight Infections

Nowadays, most parents insist that their children wash their hands before eating, and most children understand why this is important. They must wash up so they do not ingest germs—tiny living things so small they cannot be seen by the naked eye. Children know that germs can make them sick. Yet this basic knowledge, now widely known even among very young children, was hidden from the greatest minds of ancient and medieval times. Microscopes did not yet exist, so no one knew there were such things as germs.

Although doctors in ancient times did not know about germs, they did know that some diseases were contagious. During epidemics, they would separate the sick people from the healthy people in an attempt to halt the disease's progress. The doctors also noticed that people who had certain diseases became immune to them afterward.

Sometime during the Middle Ages, the Chinese and the Turks developed a way of protecting people against smallpox. The Chinese gave healthy people smallpox by blowing dust from the scabs of smallpox victims into their nostrils. The Turks rubbed this same powder into a scratch on the healthy patient's arm. Both the Chinese and the Turks used powder from the scabs of people who had relatively mild cases of smallpox, hoping that the smallpox cases it induced in the previously healthy patients would also be mild. This exposure would also protect patients from future infections of stronger strains of the virus. This technique is called inoculation.

In 1757, a Scottish physician named Francis Home tried to adapt the technique of inoculation to measles. He took blood from measles patients and injected it into healthy children, hoping to provide them with immunity from the disease without making them sick. His injection did give the healthy children measles, but their resulting illnesses were not any milder than they would have been if they spent time around a sneezing measles patient. There was no practical advantage to Home's treatment.

In 1788, Edward Jenner, an English physician, proved that he could make people permanently immune to smallpox by inoculating healthy individuals with a much milder illness called cowpox. He called his new method vaccination (from a word meaning "from cows"). The word "vaccine" has come to refer to any substance doctors use to provide a patient with immunity from a disease.

By this time, the microscope had been invented. Scientists and curious amateurs were busy using it to investigate the previously unknown world of microbes—living organisms too small to see with the naked eye. Still, the connection between microbes and diseases had yet to be established. In any case, the

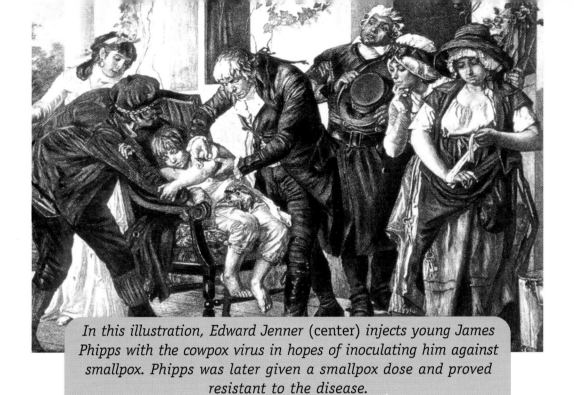

In this illustration, Edward Jenner (center) injects young James Phipps with the cowpox virus in hopes of inoculating him against smallpox. Phipps was later given a smallpox dose and proved resistant to the disease.

measles virus was far too small to be seen by the microscopes of Jenner's day.

The Germ Theory of Disease

The modern study of infectious diseases began in the late 1800s with the efforts of two scientists, Louis Pasteur in France and Robert Koch in Germany. Working separately, Pasteur and Koch established what has come to be known as the germ theory of disease. In the 1800s, doctors had many theories about the cause of infectious diseases. One of the most popular was that they were spread by "bad air." As a result, hospitals were designed for good ventilation rather than cleanliness. The possibility that microorganisms such as germs caused disease had been suggested but not yet proven.

Pasteur and Koch established the germ theory as fact. According to the germ theory, microbes are the primary cause of infectious disease, and each specific type of microbe causes a particular disease. Microbes reproduce very quickly. They travel from person to person through the air (when sick people cough or sneeze) or through physical contact. When they get inside a new victim's body, they reproduce and cause damage and illness, the type of which depends on the particular kind of microbe that has invaded the person.

Koch concentrated his studies on a common type of microbe called bacteria. While most bacteria are harmless to human beings, there are a few that cause diseases such as tuberculosis (a potentially fatal lung disease), cholera (a severe disease of the digestive system), and anthrax (a deadly lung infection). Koch proved the truth of the germ theory by growing a particular kind of bacteria outside the body, separating it from other bacteria, and using the isolated bacteria to infect previously healthy laboratory animals who soon became ill. Koch's groundbreaking work proved that the bacteria many researchers had found in sick animals were the cause of their diseases and not just a symptom or side effect of these diseases.

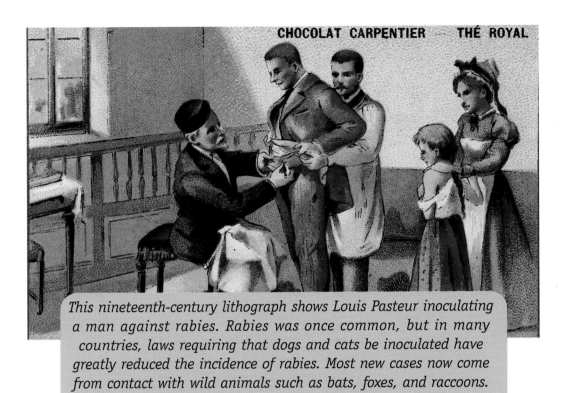

This nineteenth-century lithograph shows Louis Pasteur inoculating a man against rabies. Rabies was once common, but in many countries, laws requiring that dogs and cats be inoculated have greatly reduced the incidence of rabies. Most new cases now come from contact with wild animals such as bats, foxes, and raccoons.

While Koch worked with microbes that were large enough to be seen under his microscope, Pasteur worked with both large organisms and with creatures that were far too small to be seen with the microscopes of his day—viruses. These weakened germs were then injected into healthy animals to protect them against stronger forms of the diseases they caused. In this way, Pasteur created the first new vaccines since Jenner's time. This technique would one day be applied to the development of a vaccine against measles.

One of the early vaccines Pasteur developed gave people immunity to rabies, a fatal disease that affects animals, including human beings. Although Pasteur was certain that a microbe of some kind was the cause of rabies, he could not find one under the microscope. He guessed (correctly, as later researchers proved) that this was because it was simply too small to be seen even under a microscope. He referred to the disease agent as a "virus," from the Greek word for "poison."

The Discovery of Viruses

In 1892, a Russian scientist named Dmitri Ivanovski proved that a disease infecting a tobacco plant was caused by a microbe too small to be a bacterium. Building on Ivanovski's work, Martinus Beijerinck, a scientist working in the Netherlands, showed that the disease was caused by an infectious agent that could not reproduce itself independently but could multiply only by infecting tobacco leaves. The strange new creature was dubbed the tobacco mosaic virus, and the science of virology was born.

Some researchers began to apply this new knowledge to the study of measles. Their first question was whether measles was caused by a relatively large microbe, like a bacterium, or instead by one of those extremely tiny disease agents—viruses—that scientists were just beginning to learn about. The evidence that measles was caused by a virus grew slowly as bacteriologists looked for a measles bacterium and could not find one. By 1921, two scientists, James Trask and Francis Blake, had shown that a fluid completely free of any visible microbe could still transmit measles. For this reason, they concluded that measles was probably transmitted by a virus. At this point, however, no one had seen one of these incredibly tiny creatures. The existence of viruses was still only a theory that had yet to be proven.

Making the Measles Virus Visible

Proof of the existence of viruses would not come until the invention of the electron microscope in 1933. The electron microscope produces enlarged images of microscopic objects by focusing a beam of electrons on them through an electron lens. Electrons are particles with negative electrical charges that make up part of the atom—a tiny particle that is the basic building block of all material things, including plants and animals. The extremely tiny electron particles, penetrating or bouncing off objects on a microscope slide, provide images of objects that are hundreds of thousands of times smaller than those visible in standard optical microscopes. Scientists were able to see microscopic particles in much greater detail, and they were able to see many infinitesimal objects they had never seen before.

In 1952, with the help of the electron microscope, researchers in Texas became the first scientists to see a measles virus with their own eyes. The measles virus was round and measured around 200 nanometers—200 billionths of a meter—from end to end. It was hundreds of times smaller than a bacterium. A picture was taken of the infinitesimally small killer that had helped change the course of history, and for the first time ever, people were able to see the measles virus close up.

A London scientist prepares to examine a virus under an electron microscope in 1950. These microscopes have revolutionized the field of disease research.

4

FROM VIRUS TO VACCINE

In the early 1960s, American scientist Dr. John Enders developed the vaccine for measles. Thanks to his work, measles has become a rare disease in the United States and throughout most of the Northern Hemisphere. To understand the extent of this achievement, it helps to understand a little about the mysterious, incredibly tiny creatures known as viruses.

Viruses

Scientists are not even sure whether it is correct to say that viruses are "living" things, since viruses do not meet most of the criteria that we usually think of as constituting life. Unlike larger microbes such as bacteria and yeast,

38

viruses cannot digest food, reproduce, or manufacture chemicals on their own. Instead, they invade the cells of other living creatures—the cells of a plant or animal—and get those other cells to do the work for them. For example, when you have a cold, it is because a virus that causes colds has invaded some of your body's cells, taken command of them, and ordered them to do the work that the virus itself is not equipped to do, such as reproduce. Like a criminal taking command of a factory, the virus forces your body cells to manufacture copies of the cold virus and spread them throughout your body. The virus does not need to be able to reproduce because your cells do that for the virus. Then these copies of the virus can enter the mucus in your sinuses. Other copies of the virus make you sneeze, and when you sneeze, you spread the virus to other people. So not only does the virus not need to be able to reproduce, it does not need to be able to propel itself, either. Your sneeze or runny nose gets the virus where it needs to go.

Some people use the term "computer virus" to describe the rogue programs that hitch a ride on e-mails or electronic files and gain access to a computer's hard drive in order to damage or destroy it. This comparison is very apt. Like a computer virus, an animal or plant virus is no more than just a set of instructions. In computer viruses, the instructions take the form of computer code. In the viruses that infect living things, the instructions take the form of a genetic code, the blueprint for life that is found in all living things. The virus's genetic code can take the form of the acids DNA (deoxyribonucleic acid), which controls heredity, or RNA (ribonucleic acid), which controls a cell's chemical activity. The code gives instructions to the cells the virus invades, just as a computer virus gives instructions to the computer it invades. These instructions force the body to attack itself, as the invaded cells work to spread the infection to healthy cells.

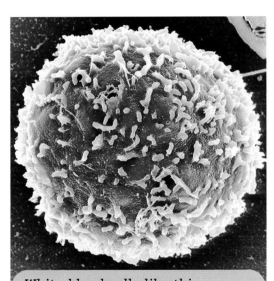

White blood cells like this one are one of the body's most important lines of defense against disease. Many vaccines work by teaching white blood cells to develop an immunity against a weakened form of a disease.

The fact that viruses are able to get other living things to do most of the work for them is the reason why, despite their extreme smallness, they are able to do such an incredible amount of damage to living things.

More than fifty years after they were first seen with the help of the electron microscope, viruses still present scientists with many mysteries. Researchers wonder, for example, how viruses came to exist in the first place, and how far back they can be traced in the history of life. Are they among the oldest living things, going back to the dawn of life on Earth? Some say they are. According to this theory, billions of years ago, simple molecules in Earth's oceans gained the ability to replicate themselves. Some of these molecules evolved into one-celled organisms, while others evolved into viruses, which then infected the one-celled organisms. Viruses evolved side by side with the one-celled organisms they infected. Another theory holds that cells appeared first. Viruses evolved out of cells that had lost so much of their genetic information over time that they became dependent on other cells for their own reproduction.

Immunity

The body's major weapon against germs is white blood cells. White blood cells fight infection by creating antibodies, which are chemicals designed to grab hold of invading germs and disable or destroy them. Antibodies are created when a white blood cell encounters a germ it has never seen before.

It can take days or even weeks for white blood cells to develop the antibodies necessary to fight a particular infection. During that period, the invading germ has the chance to multiply itself and cause illness. But once the white blood cells have succeeded in winning the battle against the invaders and killing off the virus, specialized white blood cells—sometimes called memory cells—retain copies of the antibody that is needed to fight that particular germ. If the germ ever returns, the memory cells recognize it. Your body will then quickly produce many copies of the antibody specific to that germ and wipe it out before it has a chance to make you sick again. For this reason, the immune systems of people who have had mumps, smallpox, or measles gain the ability to fight these germs in the future. Even if someone who has had measles comes into contact with the measles virus again, his or her immune system will be able to prevent a second infection with the help of the memory cells and the measles antibodies they call into action.

The idea behind a vaccine is to give people this immunity without making them sick in the first place. A vaccine is a safe, weakened, or incomplete version of a germ, which makes people only mildly sick, if at all. The weakened version of the germ still resembles the strong version closely enough to prompt our white blood cells to create antibodies. These antibodies will then protect us against the stronger and more dangerous version of the germ. Some viruses, such as those that cause cold and influenza (flu), change very quickly, developing new strains that our old antibodies cannot fight. This is why, far from getting only one cold in our lives, we continue to catch colds. This is also why doctors have to develop and administer new flu vaccines every year. Fortunately, many dangerous germs are much less prone to change than cold and flu viruses. For this reason, vaccines have turned out to be a very effective way of preventing the diseases these germs cause.

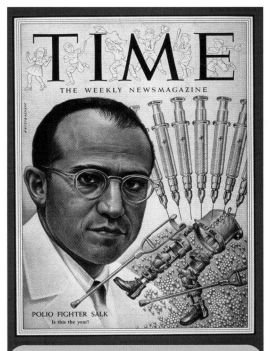

This Time *magazine cover from 1954 celebrates the achievements of Jonas Salk in finding a vaccine for polio.*

Developing the Polio Vaccine

Studying human viruses and learning how to combat them was an enormously urgent enterprise in the United States during the first half of the twentieth century. At this time, a polio epidemic was sweeping through the country. Polio, which is short for poliomyelitis, is a disease caused by a virus that infects human nerve cells. While the illness itself usually lasts a relatively short amount of time, the resulting nerve damage could be crippling or even lethal. Those the polio virus did not succeed in killing were often left handicapped for life, unable to walk, sometimes unable to breathe. Some victims of polio had to spend the rest of their lives on their backs inside a machine called an iron lung, which breathed for the patient by mechanically forcing air into and out of his or her lungs.

This young Tokyo-area polio victim struggles to walk with braces and crutches. Polio is nearly unknown now in most developed countries, thanks to the vaccines developed by Jonas Salk and other researchers.

The first great breakthrough in polio research came in the 1940s, when three American scientists —John Enders, Frederick Robbins, and Thomas

Weller—succeeded in isolating and growing the polio virus in human tissue outside the body. Their work made it possible for another scientist, Jonas Salk, to develop a vaccine for the disease in 1952.

John Enders and the Measles Vaccine

Throughout the 1950s, John Enders used the methods he developed through his polio research to also isolate the measles virus. Once he was able to do so, he turned his attention to developing a vaccine that would provide people with immunity to measles. Using the vaccination techniques

John Enders, above, won the Nobel Prize for his work on a polio vaccine, but was also well known for his measles vaccine research.

originally developed by Louis Pasteur (though in a much more complex form), Enders and his fellow researchers weakened the measles virus by passing it repeatedly through a wide variety of tissues, including those from human kidney cells and chicken embryos.

Enders and his team succeeded in creating a measles vaccine in 1963, and it was soon licensed for use in the United States. When it was given to patients, however, this vaccine made some people sick, so research continued. By 1965, scientists had succeeded in greatly reducing the number of bad reactions the vaccine caused. Yet to this day the vaccine is still not entirely safe. It is inevitable that, out of the millions of people who are given vaccines each year, some recipients will become seriously ill. A very small number may even die. Given the enormous number of lives that have been saved through prevention of deadly infections, however, public health officials, doctors, and society at large have generally considered vaccination an acceptable risk.

With the introduction of every new vaccine, health officials have to weigh the dangers and benefits and decide whether to make the vaccine available. The decision to license a vaccine is made by comparing the risk of a small number of people becoming ill or even dying following vaccination with the risk of repeated outbreaks of potentially deadly diseases occurring without the use of vaccinations. In nearly every instance, the opportunity to preserve the health of the many has outweighed concern over dangers to the few.

5

THE GLOBAL WAR AGAINST MEASLES

In the early 1960s, family doctors began to offer the measles vaccine to children whose parents wished to make their kids immune to the disease without having to actually come down with it first. Between 1963 and 1965, most measles vaccinations were given to children in relatively wealthy suburban neighborhoods. This was mainly because doctors charged parents a fee to vaccinate their children. By and large, the children of poorer families were not getting measles vaccinations, and public health officials began to wonder if this was fair. The Centers for Disease Control and Prevention (CDC) began to study the problem.

In 1966, the CDC made an announcement that viewed measles from a new perspective. It was possible, the CDC said, to completely eradicate—or stomp out—measles in the United States. Doing so would involve a massive vaccination program that would attempt to provide virtually every child in the United States with the measles vaccine. To accomplish this ambitious goal, the CDC recommended giving vaccinations as a matter of routine to all babies at one year of age. In addition, at the outset of the program, all five-year-olds who had not yet received a measles vaccine would be given one.

Vaccinating America

In practice, the CDC realized it could not vaccinate every American child. Some children are hardly ever taken to the doctor, either because of a shortage of local medical services, a lack of health insurance or cash, religious objections, or fears about medical procedures or doctors created by a lack of information about and experience with health care. In addition, some parents believe vaccinations are either ineffective or downright harmful, and no one can be forced to get a vaccination who does not want one. Even so, the CDC estimated that if between 90 and 95 percent of children were vaccinated, eventually there would not be enough unvaccinated people in the United States for the measles virus to sustain itself. Measles would cease to be endemic in the United States.

This is what eventually happened, though it took much longer to achieve than the CDC had at first expected. In 1962, the United States Congress voted to spend money to provide free measles vaccinations. Between 1966 and 1968, 19.5 million doses of the measles vaccine were given to children in the United States. Immediately, the number of measles cases went down. In 1962, the year before the measles vaccine was introduced, there were 481,530 cases of measles reported in the United States. In 1968, there were only 22,231—about one-twentieth of the number in 1962.

Measles cases began to rise again in the late 1970s, after federal funds for immunization programs were cut. In response, the U.S. government launched a new vaccination campaign intended to eliminate measles. As part of this campaign, starting in 1978, doctors in the United States began giving children a combined vaccine that protected against measles, mumps (a viral infection that causes fever and swelling of the glands near the ear), and rubella (German measles, a milder form of measles that is damaging to fetuses in the early stages of pregnancy).

By the late 1990s, the campaign against measles in the United States had achieved its goal. Measles was no longer an endemic disease in the United

States. Canada, the United Kingdom, and many other countries in the developed world have introduced similar vaccination programs with similarly good results.

Can Measles Be Wiped Out Worldwide?

Thanks to a vaccine, smallpox was eradicated in the United States in 1949. The last recorded case of naturally occurring smallpox was in 1977 in Somalia, on the horn of Africa. Since smallpox cannot exist in animals and cannot survive for more than about twenty-four hours outside the human body, a period in which no new cases are reported in a given area indicates that smallpox has been eradicated there. Since no new cases were reported worldwide after 1977, smallpox was declared extinct in 1980 by the World Health Organization (WHO).

The first disease for which a vaccination was invented became the first disease to be wiped out worldwide. Today, smallpox exists only in laboratories, and scientists are debating whether the samples that exist should simply be destroyed, especially since there are growing fears that terrorists could get their hands on the smallpox virus and reintroduce the deadly disease to the world.

Actress Jane Seymour (center, in white hat) *helps administer measles vaccinations to children in Nairobi, Kenya, in 2002. Seymour was publicizing a measles initiative by the Red Cross organization, of which she is a cabinet member. The initiative seeks to vaccinate all Kenyan children under the age of fifteen by 2007.*

Could measles also be eradicated one day, reduced to a laboratory specimen as smallpox was? And if it can be, would it be worth the effort? International public health officials believe that it would be both possible and worthwhile to wipe out measles. Measles and smallpox used to travel together, causing terrible damage to humanity; it would be very appropriate for measles to share extinction with smallpox. Besides, public health officials point to special characteristics of measles that would make wiping it out far easier. Like smallpox and unlike the cold or flu viruses, measles is a virus that does not change very much over time. As a result, doctors would only have to wipe out two strains of the virus—measles and German measles, or rubella.

Also like smallpox, measles is an easy disease to recognize, due mainly to the rash that is its most obvious symptom. So when a measles epidemic hits a community, people quickly become aware of it. This is important because in order to wipe out a disease, you have to be able to figure out where the disease still exists. When trying to eradicate smallpox, health workers used to rush to the spot where a new small-pox case was reported and quickly vaccinate everyone in the area so that the disease had no one new to infect. This same approach could be taken with measles as well.

Stamping out measles worldwide would be worth the effort because the disease is still a major killer in the parts of the world where it is widespread. However, measles eradication faces some special obstacles that smallpox eradication did not. For one thing, the danger a measles outbreak poses is differ-ent in different parts of the world. In most areas of the Northern Hemisphere—where nations tend to be developed and have good health care—the risk of severe illness or death with measles infection is low. As a result, there is little sense of urgency surround-ing the issue of eradicating the disease in the far more impoverished and vulnerable nations of the Southern Hemisphere. When the developed world backed the eradication of the far more deadly disease smallpox, it did so partly out of self-interest. As long as smallpox existed, it could always come back and cause a deadly epidemic in England, Japan, or the United States. By contrast, measles poses much less danger in well-off countries than smallpox did, even though it continues to be a great killer in poor countries.

Another obstacle to measles eradication is the poverty and political chaos in some of the African nations where most of the work on measles eradication will have to be done. For example, Somalia, the place where the last smallpox case was found in the 1970s, has been in a state of anarchy with no central government for more than fifteen years. There is no single Somali government to assist World Health Organization doctors in getting vaccinations to the people who need them. For the same reason, it is also very hard to pinpoint the location of measles outbreaks because, without a central government, little information is gathered by public health officials. Since some of these developing nations are also war-torn, it would even be difficult to ensure the safety of the doctors who would volunteer to administer the vaccination program. War, hunger, and disease have often been linked throughout history. It may be that these problems, so often found together, will have to be solved together as well.

In any case, public health officials are determined to try. In October 2003, health officials from sixty countries met in Cape Town, South Africa, and pledged to launch a new campaign to eradicate measles. The campaign is called the Global Measles Partnership and is led by the United Nations International Children's Emergency Fund (UNICEF), the WHO, the CDC, and the Red Cross. The partnership estimates that the measles eradication program will cost between $600 million and $700 million through 2008. Measles killed 875,000 people, most of them children, in 1999. If there is a reasonably safe opportunity to reduce the death toll to zero and banish the measles virus forever, it seems like it must be taken.

GLOSSARY

antibiotics A class of drugs that kills bacteria.

bacterium A member of a class of single-celled microorganisms, some of which cause infections and disease in animals and humans. The plural of "bacterium" is "bacteria."

bronchitis An inflammation and congestion of the bronchial tubes that lead into the lungs.

DNA Deoxyribonucleic acid, the complex molecule that contains the genetic code, or "blueprint," that living things use to reproduce themselves.

electron microscope A microscope that works by focusing beams of electrons, making it possible to produce images of objects hundreds of thousands of times smaller than those visible under an optical microscope.

endemic Relating to a disease that is always present within a given area or population.

epidemic A more or less sudden, widespread outbreak of a disease.

eradicate To get rid of or completely destroy.

immune system The body system that helps fight off infection.

microbe A living thing so small that it cannot be seen with the naked eye.

nanometer A linear measurement equaling a billionth of a meter.

optical microscope A microscope that works by bending light with the help of lenses or mirrors.

pneumonia An infection and/or inflammation of the lung tissue.

poliomyelitis Polio; a virus that infects human nerve cells.

prevalent Widespread.

seizures Random firings of cells in the nervous system, often resulting in sudden, involuntary movements of the muscles or in hallucinations.

vaccine A substance that stimulates the immune system, providing protection against infection.

virus A member of a class of extremely tiny disease-causing agents that can perform the basic functions of life only when they invade a living cell.

FOR MORE INFORMATION

Centers for Disease Control and Prevention (CDC)
1600 Clifton Road
Atlanta, GA 30333
(404) 639-3311 or (800) 311-3435
Web site: http://www.cdc.gov/ncidod

National Institutes of Health (NIH)
9000 Rockville Pike
Bethesda, MD 20892
(301) 496-4000
Web site: http://www.nih.gov

National Network for Immunization Information
301 University Boulevard, CH 2.218
Galveston, TX 77555
(409) 772-0199
Web site: http://www.immunizationinfo.org

U.S. National Library of Medicine
8600 Rockville Pike
Bethesda, MD 20894
Web site: http://www.nlm.nih.gov

World Health Organization (WHO)
525 23rd Street NW
Washington, DC 20037
(202) 974-3000
Web site: http://www.who.int/en

In Canada

Health Canada
A.L. 0900C2
Ottawa, Ontario, K1A 0K9
(613) 957-2991 or (800) 267-1245
Web site: http://www.hc-sc.gc.ca/english

Web Sites

Due to the changing nature of Internet links, the
Rosen Publishing Group, Inc., has developed an
online list of Web sites related to the subject of this
book. This site is updated regularly. Please use this
link to access the list:

http://www.rosenlinks.com/epid/meas

FOR FURTHER READING

De Kruif, Paul, and F. Gonzales-Cruissi. *Microbe Hunters*. New York: Harvest Books, 2002.

Hawkins, Trisha. *Everything You Need to Know About Measles and Rubella*. New York: The Rosen Publishing Group, Inc., 2001.

Hyde, Margaret O., and Elizabeth H. Forsyth, MD. *Vaccinations: From Smallpox to Cancer*. New York: Franklin Watts, 2000.

Jakab, E. A. M. *Louis Pasteur: Hunting Killer Germs*. New York: McGraw Hill/Contemporary Books, 2000.

Zimmerman, B. E., and D. J. Zimmerman. *Killer Germs: Microbes and Diseases That Threaten Humanity*. Chicago: Contemporary Books, 1996.

BIBLIOGRAPHY

Bellenir, Karen, and Peter D. Dresser, eds. *Contagious and Non-Contagious Infectious Diseases Sourcebook*. Detroit: Omnigraphics, Inc., 1995.

Brothwell, Don R. *Diseases in Antiquity: A Survey of the Diseases, Injuries, and Surgery of Early Populations*. New York: Thomas Publishing Co., 1967.

Cliff, Andrew David, P. Haggett, and M. Smallman-Raynor. *Measles: An Historical Geography of a Major Human Viral Disease, from Global Expansion to Local Retreat, 1840–1990*. Oxford, England: Blackwell Reference, 1993.

Cook, Noble David, and N. George Lovell. *Secret Judgments of God: Old World Disease in Colonial Spanish America*. Tulsa, OK: University of Oklahoma Press, 1991.

Curtin, Philip D. *Death by Migration: Europe's Encounter with the Tropical World in the Nineteenth Century*. Cambridge, England: Cambridge University Press, 1989.

"Epidemics." The USGenWeb Project. 1999–2000. Retrieved January 2004 (http://www.usgenweb.org/researchers/epidemics.html).

Institute of Medicine. *Immunization Safety Review: Measles-Mumps-Rubella Vaccine and Autism*. Washington, DC: National Academy Press, 2001.

Papania, Mark. "Measles (Rubeola)." National Center for Infectious Diseases Travelers' Health. 2003–2004. Retrieved January 2004 (http://www.cdc.gov/travel/diseases/measles.htm).

INDEX

CREDITS

About the Author

Maxine Rosaler is a freelance author living in New York City.

Photo Credits